SUN SUN GO AWAY
and other poems

by Georgia Spanos

with illustrations by
Maddison Kitching

/

"I was lucky enough to read Georgia's poems while travelling up the Caribbean coast of Mexico. I had left my sketchbook with a gallery in Mexico City and had limited materials. As I passed through different towns, I collected old receipts, little notes, and pieces of rubbish to paint on. The artworks in this book are ripples of these poems, the materials I found, and the places they were made."

- Maddison Kitching, Guadalajara, May 2023

An Unsettling Screech

We can hear it
somewhere we don't know
but here

its screech echoes like a scream
it's frustrating
locality a mystery

'turn on the light' she plots
'don't move' she orders
'right there' she finds
'your shoe' she demands

but still
uncaptured

'what does it need' I ask
'what from us' I wonder
'how can we help' I propose
'enough' she sighs
we fall

surrender to exhaustion
accepting camp wounds ahead

and then
its unsettling screech
sings us calmly
to
sleep

Do you recall
how you thought
back then?
'Hi dear'
But now you can't
breathe again
It's time to land
somewhere new
But when your toes touch the sea
they turn purple
and blue
Oh—to feel shrew
in this place new
No one will stop breathing if they see your face
You're a squid in the weeds
tangled up in space
So you get on your way
and fly back to that day
'There are more than 500 species of squid'
You say

The Squabbling Squid

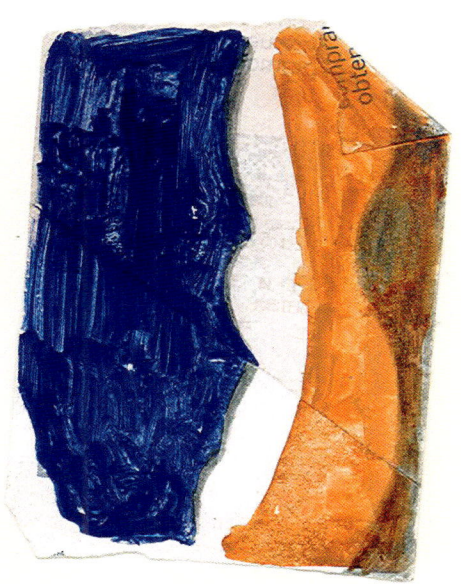
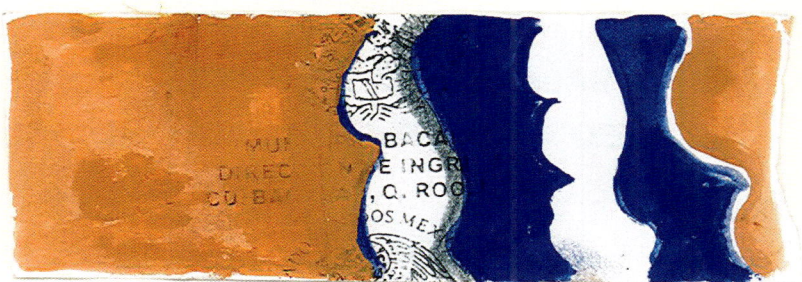

Long Distance

My phone is my boyfriend
I'm in love with my phone

You're out with the people
But when you get home

You lie with your love
You lie with your phone

And when your phone dies
You're single again

It's on and it's ringing
Your single life ends

Dance Around the Tent

It's freezing in here
and you're crazy—insane

even though the music has stopped
you're dancing still
as if it has not

BLAST

zip
open
close

head first you fly
take off your clothes

you smell
puffed
and now you're done

you wrap two hands
and squeeze my thumb

it's archaic to hold
for closeness—just that

for the touch of wisdom
wings betrayal

from the young
… and the stupid

I'm flying
Flipping

Slapped on month-heated stones

I'd rather be snug in butter
You know?

My once-known now scattered
This must be what lonely feels

And so here I lie
Lonely at last

Watching souls miss my head
Not hidden instead

The Street Slug

Sun Sun Go Away

Why does everyone

Talk about the sun?

Where it's been?

When it will come

It's always there

You just can't see

It's sitting there

Comfortably

I'm not sure, just get out, and swim
'Right here?' my trembling voice utters
Yes get out, run, and swim
She passes me goggles
Keep going… going… yes… keep going
'More?' I cry
Yes, don't worry it's not jellyfish season
… Watch out for that jellyfish
She laughs
And feels a little guilty
'That was really nice' I smile, exasperated
Come on let's get coffee
She springs
And carries on

Just Swim

Web Mind

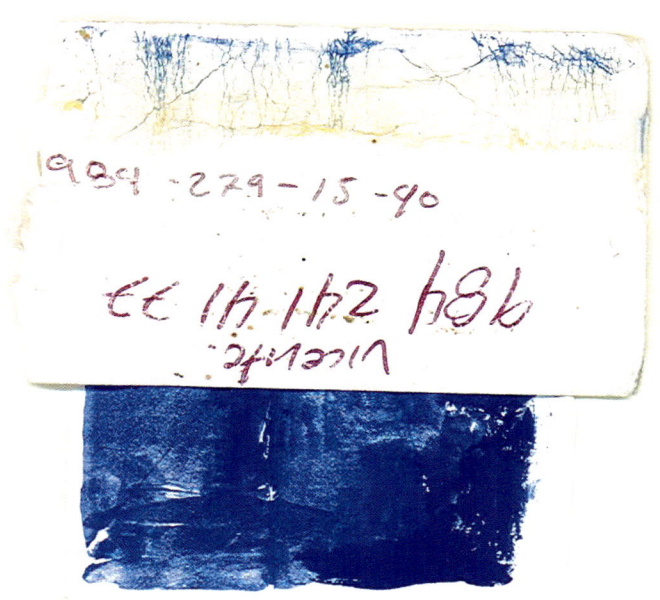

If I were a date
I would split in two
The saxophone colours around her
Goodnight

I was told once before
To count the colours as they greet
And when they fuse
The notes then soft

But If I were a morning
She glimmers through glimpse
The notes still art
I split in three

Chaos at the Onsen

Hello ma'am
You're late…

Hello
puff

Yes sorry
puff

It took me a while to get here
puff puff

It's okay ma'am
You still have 40 minutes

Perfect, because I'm in a hour park
I relieve

But ma'am
Your shiatsu massage is right after…

Oh
I pause

Can I quickly move my car after then?
and raise a solution

Yes ma'am
But you will be in your onsen clothes

That's okay
I smile

… I really like them

Take off your mask

it's worn and it fades,

now all can see

you unravelling.

Don't worry I'll help

you come back to the place,

where you first saw that thing

and masked up your face

Masked Now

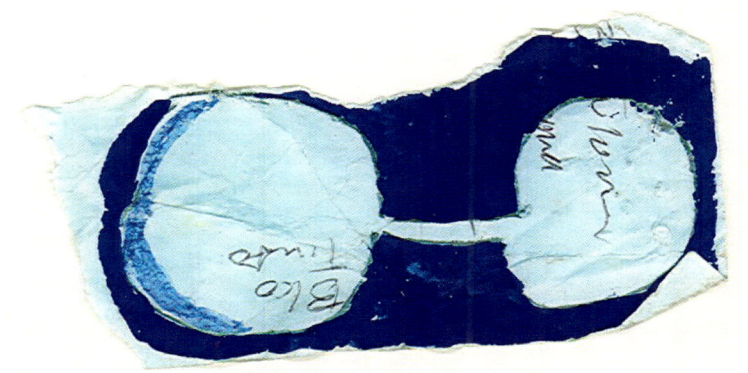

book design by
Nataliya Vitorovich